iWork for iPad: Sudden

SERVICE

By Richard Baker

Officially, this book is published by Baker Publications, which is another name I go by. Unlike so many other publishers these days, it is not a division of anything else.

I'd add some Library of Congress catalog data here, except that the Library of Congress hasn't gotten around to cataloging it.

Contents

Introduction:

Rural diners used to post signs promising "Sudden Service." Some probably still do. This book is intended to offer much the same thing: quick access to help you get an immediate job done using iWork for the iPad. You can read it end to end. But you'll often find it more useful as a handy reference to help you get the most from the iPad versions of Pages, Numbers, and Keynote. In fact, you can carry this book in electronic form, right on the iPad itself.

Check the Contents for the job you need to do; then, you can jump directly to that section. Cross-references lead you to other helpful information.

Working with the iPad can be an interesting, productive experience. Enjoy.

Getting acquainted

The iPad is a wonderful instrument, but it lacks some of the features of its Mac-based brethren.

You can say the same about the iPad version of the iWork collection. The iPad editions take advantage of the system's unique features, but they also must adapt to the tablet's limitations. These include the lack of a mouse and only a limited-duty keyboard.

Notably, iWork version 5 for the Mac has been made much more like the IOS version that appears on the iPad. The change has been controversial. Many professional-level features have been removed from the Mac version.

Both iPad and Mac editions of the iWork applications start by offering selections of layout templates for a new document, spreadsheet or presentation.

On the iPad, you can start with a blank document, or you can choose templates for longer documents like reports and term papers. Most of the available templates, though, are for shorter documents like fliers and posters. The selection reinforces the iPad version's expected role, creating shorter, more visual documents.

The other two applications follow the same pattern. Compared with their Mac versions, there are fewer templates, also called themes, and each template has fewer sample page layouts.

1

You also may find more often than you like that a font you used in the Mac version is not available on the iPad.

Then, there is the virtual keyboard that appears on-screen whenever there is something to be typed. It works better than you might expect, but it does take some getting used to.

Within those limits, though, the iPad may prove to be surprisingly versatile. Collectively, it includes an assortment of useful tools that are literally at your fingertips. With these features, the iWork applications offer enough flexibility and portability to serve as valuable creative devices in its own right.

Another limitation: the iPad is not well equipped to print your finished documents. It needs the help of a specially-equipped printer or a desktop computer.

What's on the screen?

When you open an iWork application on the iPad, you have your choice of landscape or portrait mode. Switching between the two is a matter of turning the iPad to the configuration you want. Though easy to execute, the choice is often a trade-off. In portrait mode, you can see a fair-sized screen area, but the keyboard is on the tiny side.

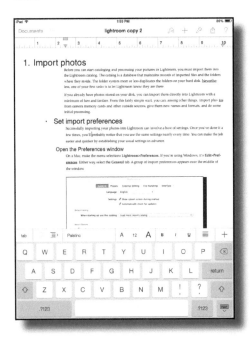

In landscape mode, the on-screen keyboard is larger and easier to use, but this comes at the expense of display space.

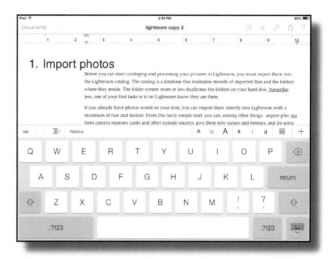

Either way, a **toolbar** stretches across the top of the screen. It offers buttons you can use to accomplish common tasks:

- **Documents**. Use this button to create a new document or open an existing one.

- **Undo**. Tap this button to undo a change. Touch and hold it to redo your action.

- **Style** (the paint brush button). Style text, format lists, and set up page layouts.

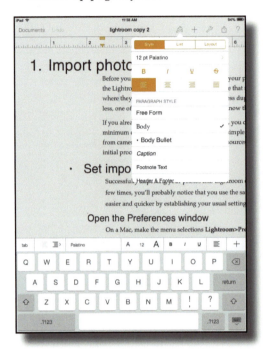

- **Insert**. Include photos, shapes, tables, and charts.

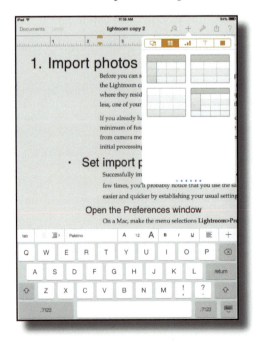

- **Tools** (the wrench symbol). Apply settings and use resources.

Touchscreen basics

The iWork applications bring some new terms to the process. In particular, they depend heavily on finger gestures (no, not that kind). They include:

- **Tap**. Using a single finger, tap on the screen. You can use this gesture to select an object or to activate a button. This is the equivalent of clicking with a mouse.

In Keynote, you can tap on a slide presentation to advance to the next slide.

- **Two-finger tap**. Tap with two fingers simultaneously to select an entire paragraph of text. This is the equivalent of double-clicking with a mouse.

- **Pinch**. Place two fingers on the screen, and pinch them together. This zooms out and reduces the size of the display.

- **Pinch open**. There's no easy term for this. Place two fingers on the screen, and spread them apart. This has the effect of zooming in on the display.

- **Scroll**. Slide your finger up or down to scroll through a display. To move more quickly, you can rapidly flick your finger across the screen.

Manipulate objects

With the help of these gestures, you can move and rotate the objects on the screen. These include shapes, photos, movies, and text boxes. You can use these techniques:

- **Drag**. You can move an object by touching it and dragging it across the screen. You can resize it by dragging one of its blue selection handles.

- **Constrained drag**. Touch the screen with one finger, and drag with the other hand. Use this method to drag in a straight line, horizontally, vertically, or at a 45-degree angle.

- **Rotate**. Place two fingers on the object, and turn them.

- **Select multiple objects.** Touch one object on the screen, then tap others you want to select.

PAGES

Chapter 1. Build and manage documents

The basic purpose of Pages, both the Mac and iPad editions, is to create and manage documents. These can include letters, brochures, articles, reports, white papers, off-white papers, you name it.

In all likelihood, the first thing you probably will want to do is to open or create a document so you can work on it. Finding an existing document, or creating a new one are elementary tasks. Accomplishing them is a little bit challenging. Not a lot more, but a little.

1. Open an existing document

If you previously closed Pages with an open document, the program should reopen it for you. Otherwise, you can tap on the Documents button in the upper left-hand corner of the screen. You should see a display of your existing documents.

Tap on a document, and it opens immediately.

2. Build a new document from a template

To start a new document, you must apply a template. Even if you want to start with a blank piece of paper, you must start with a Blank template. Then, you can go about adding or replacing text and graphics.

Display the templates

This is also true of the Mac version of Pages.

In the upper left-hand corner, tap on the Plus sign. This opens a window that includes the option Create Document.

Tap on **Create Document**, and a display of available templates opens.

Pick a template

Scroll down, if necessary, to find a template that fits the type of document you want to create. Tap on that template, and a new document opens with the selected layout.

When picking a template, look for an appropriate design. Ignore the subject matter; you'll want to use your own, anyway.

If you've chosen a blank template, you can start typing right away. Otherwise, you'll undoubtedly notice some content that really doesn't apply: Latin oratory and pictures of people you've never seen before. This is placeholder content you can replace with more relevant material of your own. For more on this, see ""4. *Replace placeholder text*"" and "5. *Replace placeholder pictures*"

3. Navigate through a document

Given the iPad's limited screen area, the display can get cluttered in a hurry. Pages normally displays your document one page at a time.

Go to a selected page

To scroll to a different page, touch the right-hand edge of the screen. Hold it for a moment until a navigator appears. It looks something like a magnifying glass; a page number appears in the pointer.

Drag the navigator up or down until you find the page you want. Lift your finger, and the document scrolls to that page.

Go back to the top

Tap on the status bar at the extreme top of the screen. You will jump directly to the document's first page.

4. Replace placeholder text

If you're building a document from a template, you'll see plenty of things you want to replace.

First, undoubtedly, is the Latin text. It's from a famous oration by the Roman Cicero, but that doesn't do much to make it suitable for your purposes.

Select the text

Since the placeholder text is of little use for anything else, a single tap selects the entire block of text. Double-tapping selects a paragraph like the line of text that displays the price of the house.

Type the new text

Once you've selected text, you also can cut, copy, and paste. For more details, see "7. Select a word or several".

Type the text you want to use instead. That's it. Your new text appears in the document.

5. Replace placeholder pictures

You also can replace the placeholder pictures with those of your choosing.

Select the picture

In the lower right-hand corner of each placeholder picture is an editing symbol.

Tap on that symbol. Pictures on the iPad are arranged into albums, and a list of these albums opens.

Tap on the album that contains the picture you want to insert. The pictures in that album are displayed.

Tap on the picture you want to include. It is automatically added to the document, replacing the placeholder picture.

6. Organize documents in folders

The iPad doesn't readily recognize the system of folders that desktop users find familiar. Pages makes up for that lack by providing its own system of folders. If you have multiple documents you want to group together—say sections of a report—you can create a folder for them in Pages.

Switch to edit view

In the **Documents** view, tap on the **Edit** button in the upper right-hand corner. The documents will begin to jiggle.

You can also open the edit view by touching and holding any of the displayed documents.

Drag the documents into position

While they are jiggling, touch the photos you want to include in the folder. The selected photos display colored borders.

Touch one of the selected photos. All the selected photos will appear to gather themselves under this photo. Drag them to another document. Pages creates a folder that

contains all the selected photos, including the destina-
tion photo.

Rename the folder

The resulting folder bears the unexciting name **Folder**. You'll probably want something more descriptive. Tap on the name of the folder, and you can enter the name of your choice.

Chapter 2. Make and use selections

Selecting text isn't one of the iPad's greatest features. It requires precise use of your fingertips, and for most of us, the fingertips aren't exactly precision instruments. Making an accurate selection requires tapping, slipping, sliding and gliding in exactly the right places. You can do it, but it probably will take some practice.

7. Select a word or several

A stylus can help greatly.

The easiest way to select a word is to double-tap on it. This is roughly the same thing as double-clicking with a mouse. In the same vein, triple-tapping selects a paragraph.

But what if you want to select a phrase or a sentence? To do that requires a more gentle touch.

Insert an insertion point

Take the supposedly simple task of placing the insertion point at the precise location where you want to add or edit some text. The basic technique is to tap at the place where you want the insertion point to appear.

Chances are, this approach didn't place the bar exactly where you wanted. You probably have to move it around some. To do this, place your finger on the line of text near the insertion point; you don't have to be precise right now. Hold it until a magnifying glass appears.

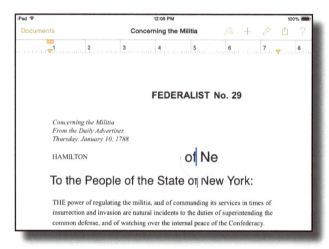

Now, slide your finger along the line of text, using the magnifier as a guide. When you reach the desired spot, lift your finger. The insertion point should be right where you want it. The operative term is *should be*. Particularly when you're getting started, it will probably take more than one try.

Drag a selection

You can't place an insertion point in placeholder text. Pages selects the entire text block, assuming you'd like to replace the whole thing.

When you select a word or paragraph, handles called *drag points* appear at either side of the selection.

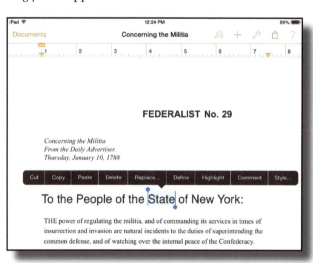

True to their name, you can move these drag points to expand or contract the selection.

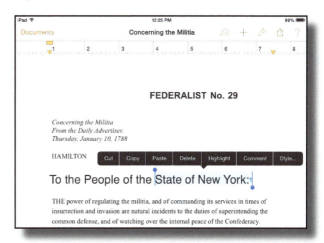

Do something with the selection

When you make a selection, a menu of options appears above it. These options include the basic tasks of cutting, copying, and pasting plus several other options.

Say you want to move the selected text somewhere else. Start by selecting the **Cut** option. Then, repeat the process of placing the selection point, this time at the place where you want to place the selected text. Or, if there's text you want to replace, select it. This time, the pop-up menu gives you a **Paste** option. Use it to place the selection in its new home.

The pop-up menu has other options including the ability to delete the selection, highlight it, or add a comment.

8. Apply styles and formatting

Pages uses an assortment of defined styles to set the type size, format, and other specifications for paragraph: larger type for a heading, for example, and a smaller font for body text. If you've started a document from one of the iPad templates, Pages offers the styles it has assigned to that template. If you've imported a document from the Mac version of Pages, the styles you used in that document are also available.

The **Style** option on the pop-up menu does not do what you might expect. It allows you to copy the style of the selected text so you can apply it somewhere else. You can't use it the other way around: to apply a different style to the selection. To see how to do that, see *8. Apply styles and formatting*

17

Apply a paragraph style

Tap the **Style** symbol in the upper right-hand corner of the screen. A list of available styles is displayed.

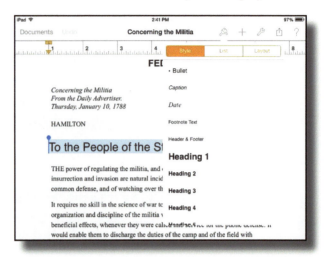

Scroll down if necessary, and tap on the style you want to use. It is applied to the selected text.

Apply local formatting

Maybe you don't want to change the format of an entire paragraph. Perhaps you just want to change a key word or phrase to italics. If so, you can use the buttons that appear at the top of the keyboard display.

Select the text you want to set in italics. Then, tap on the *I* button. The selected text changes to italics.

You also can make several other type changes from this row of buttons:

- **To insert a tab:** tap on the **Tab** button.

- **To indent the text:** tap on the indent symbol.

- **To change the typeface:** Tap on the current type face name. A list of available typefaces is displayed. Scroll through the list, if necessary, and select the face you want.

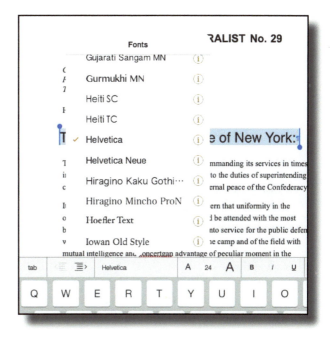

- **To make the type larger or smaller:** Tap on the type size indicator, and select a new size. Or, tap the **A** symbols on either side of the indicator to increase or reduce the type size.

- **To apply bold, italic, or underlined type:** Tap on the **B**, **I** or **U** symbol.

- **To align the text:** Tap on the **Alignment** button. From the menu that opens, select a new alignment.

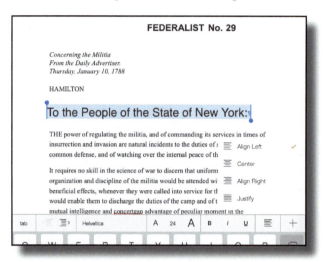

9. Set and use tab stops

The ruler at the top of the screen is the control center for aligning text and setting tab stops. It automatically appears whenever you place the insertion point within text.

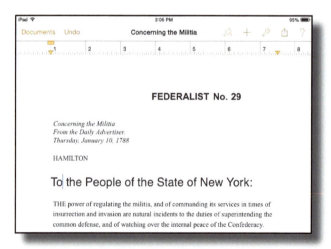

Insert a tab stop

Tap on the ruler at the point where you want to apply the tab stop. As with so many fingertip operations, the tab may not appear precisely where you want it. In that case, drag it into position; a magnifier gives you some help.

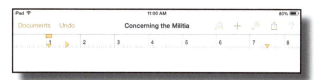

Set the alignment

To remove the tab stop, drag it down off the ruler.

Initially, Pages inserts a left-aligned tab; the left side of the affected text will line up on this tab. Its symbol on the ruler is a right- facing arrow. There are times when you will want to align the tab differently. You have these alternatives:

- Right-aligned text indicated by a right-facing arrow.

- Centered text indicated by a diamond shape.

- Decimal-aligned text indicated by a circle.

To change the alignment, double-tap on the tab, repeating until it displays the alignment you want.

Insert a tab into your text

Start with the insertion point at the place where you want to enter the tab. Then, tap on the **tab** button at the left-hand end of the keyboard ruler.

10. Set margins for a paragraph

The ruler at the top of the screen is the place to set margins as well as tab stops. For example, you can use it to indent a single paragraph, perhaps to emphasize an extended quotation.

To set the margins for an entire document, see *14. Set the margins*.

Select the paragraph

Tap in the paragraph whose margins you want to adjust.

Adjust the margins

Use the triangular buttons in the ruler to change the margins. There are two, one for each margin. As you might suspect, move the buttons inward to increase the margins; outward to reduce them.

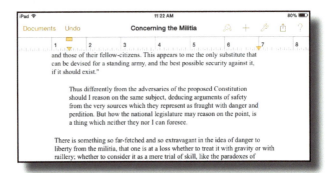

11. Adjust line spacing

Perhaps you want the lines in a paragraph to be more widely spaced. In the Toolbar, tap on the **Style** button. From the menu that opens, select **Layout**. You can use the **Line Spacing** arrows to adjust the spacing between lines.

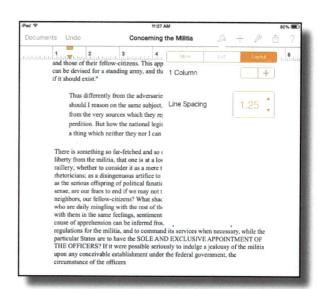

These arrows adjust the spacing typewriter- style by inserting a certain number of lines. It does not recognize the typographical practice of inserting leading to space the lines. For more sophisticated styling techniques, see *"8. Apply styles and formatting"*

If you want to format the text into two or more columns, you can also do it here.

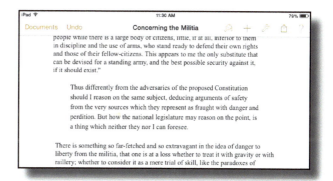

12. Set up a list

You often may want to use letters, numbers, or bullet points to identify the items in a list. You can pretty much do this as you type.

Start a list

Suppose you want to start a numbered list. Go to the place where you want to start the first item, type a 1, a period, and a space. Pages starts the list automatically.

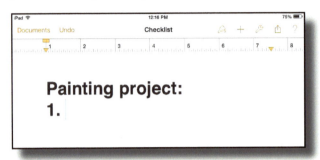

To start a lettered list captioned A, B, C and so on, start with the letter A, a period, and a space.

Type the first item in the list, then tap on **Return**. The next item is automatically labeled 2. Continue to add each item. When the list is complete, tap on **Return** twice.

Revise the numbering

This is all well and good, but after you finish the list you might decide you'd like to use letters instead of numbers. Or, perhaps you want to turn some ordinary text into a numbered list.

Select the items you want to change. Then, tap on the **Style** button on the **Toolbar**. From the menu that opens, select **List**.

A list of available list styles opens. To replace the letters with numbers, tap on **Lettered**.

You can also use this method to apply bullets. To return the list to conventional text, tap on **None**.

Chapter 3. Lay out a page

The Mac edition of Pages has a flexible variety of features for laying out a page. You can pick the paper size, set the margins, and display multiple columns. On the iPad, Pages has some of these page layout features, but not all of them.

Many of the available options also are limited. For example, the iPad edition offers only a pair of page size options, and they don't differ by much. Nevertheless, the iPad edition does cover the basics of setting up pages for the best display.

13. Set the page size

Though only a couple of page sizes are available, you can work within either of these to set margins and other specifications.

Tap on the **Tool** icon in the Toolbar. From the menu that opens, tap on **Document Setup**.

A graphic Document Setup display occupies the entire

screen.

Tap on **Change the Page Size** near the bottom of the screen. You are offered a choice of two paper sizes: the standard U.S. Letter or the slightly smaller A4.

Tap on your choice. The selected page size is displayed.

14. Set the margins

In the Document Setup display, double-headed arrows mark the four margins of the printed page. Initially, they are set for 1.25 inches on either side and 1 inch at the top and bottom. Drag any of these arrows to change the margins. Labels help you keep track of the new dimensions.

15. Insert headers and footers

The Document Setup display is also the place to insert the headers and footers that appear on the top and bottom of every page. These can include page numbers, titles, chapter headings or other information you want to present.

Insert a page number

Tap on the header or footer space. A menu gives you the opportunity to call for page numbers in that space.

A list available page number formats is displayed. Tap on the one you want to use.

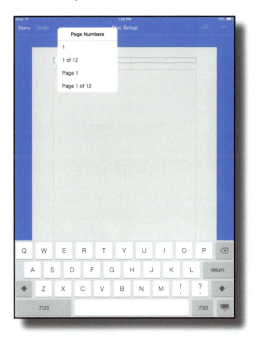

Enter header or footer text

You also can enter a text label, such as the document's title, in the header or footer space.

Tap on the header or footer. The insertion point appears in the selected label area. Type the text you want to use.

Align the entry

You can enter headers and footers that appear flush left, centered, or flush right. To select an alignment, tap on the **Style** icon; then select **Style**. Select any of the alignment symbols above the Paragraph Style heading. In this window, you also can select a type face, weight, or a preformatted style for the header or footer text.

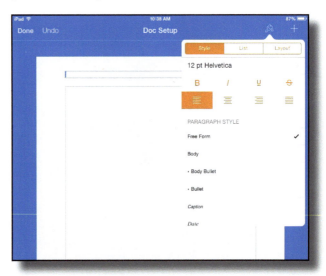

16. Insert page breaks

Suppose you have a series of headings or subheadings, and you want each to start at the top of a new page. To do this, insert page breaks at the opening of each section.

Page breaks also divide the document into sections you can format separately. For example, if you change the number of columns in a section that begins at a page break, Pages applies that format until it reaches the next page break, if there is one. Below that, you again see the original number of columns.

Insert the break

Place the insertion point where you want the page break to begin. Then, tap on the **Plus** sign above the keyboard. From the menu that opens, select **Page Break**.

The text moves to the top of a new page. You can format this text differently than the rest of the document, such as changing the number of columns.

17. Change the number of columns

Multiple columns often can make a document more readable; they help the reader out by breaking up long lines of type. You can set the number of columns for the entire document, for one or more selected paragraphs, or for a section defined by page breaks.

Identify the start

Place the insertion point where you want the new column layout to begin. The new layout will continue until the end of the document or until the next page break. Or, select the adjacent paragraphs to which you want to apply the new columns.

Set the number of columns

Tap on the **Style** icon in the upper right-hand corner of the screen; then select **Layout**. Use the **Plus** or **Minus** signs to increase or reduce the number of columns.

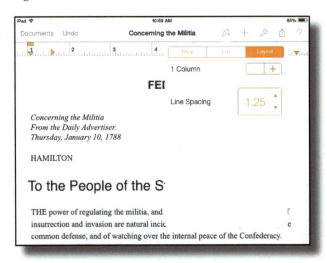

Move text to the top of the next column

You may have an item you want to move to the top of a new column. If so, place the insertion point at the beginning of the text you want to move. Tap on the **Plus** sign at the top of the keyboard, and select **Column Break.**

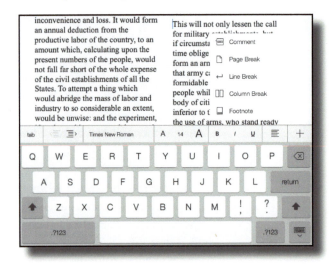

Text after the break moves to the top of the next column.

That may be on the next page.

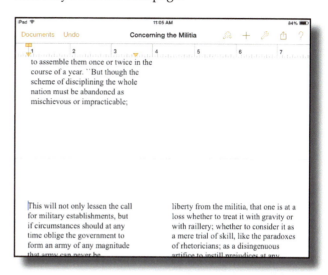

18. Insert footnotes and endnotes

Chances are, you won't try to write a grad school thesis on the iPad. Nevertheless, there are times when you might find yourself doing formal research which requires that you identify your sources in a prescribed manner. If so, you can enter footnotes and later, if you wish, convert them to endnotes.

Pick the spot

A footnote appears on the same page as its numbered reference. An endnote appears at the end of a chapter or document.

Place the insertion point where you want the footnote to appear. This is usually at the end of a sentence or paragraph. Tap on the **Plus** sign above the keyboard.

Insert the note

Tap on **Footnote**. A superscript footnote number appears at the insertion point. At the bottom of the screen, a box opens where you can type the note.

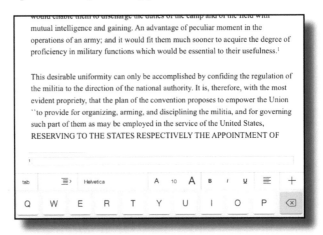

19. Change footnotes to endnotes

If you would rather use endnotes instead, you can do so at any time. Tap on any footnote in the document. Blue boxes enclose each of the notes in the document.

Select any footnote in the document. Tap on the **Style** symbol in the upper right-hand corner of the screen. A

Changes you make here apply to all the notes in the document. You can't combine footnotes and endnotes in the same document.

Footnotes menu opens.

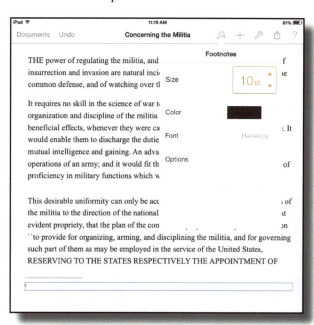

Tap on **Options**. A menu of further options opens.

You can also use this menu to change the typeface, color and size of the text used in the note.

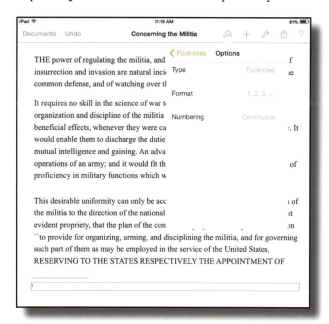

Select **Type**. You have the option of changing to End-notes or Section endnotes. Tap on your choice.

Document endnotes appear at the end of the document. Section endnotes appear at the end of a section.

Reminder: In Pages for the iPad, sections are denoted by inserted page breaks. See "16. *Insert page breaks*". When you select Section endnotes, the notes appear at the end of each section.

Chapter 4. Charts, tables and graphics

You can add text and illustrations by replacing the placeholder items in a Pages template. You also can add them to any place on any Page. Then, you can resize, reposition, and restyle them at will. You can include illustrations, movies, shapes, separate text boxes, charts and tables.

20. Add a picture to the document

You can add a picture to the document by selecting it from any of the resources in the iPad's Photos application.

Select the photo

Tap on the **Insert** button (the big Plus sign) in the toolbar. From the buttons at the top of the menu, select **Media**, the musical symbol. A list of photo resources appears.

Since the photo to be used here was recently imported, it appears twice, once in its current folder and once as the last import.

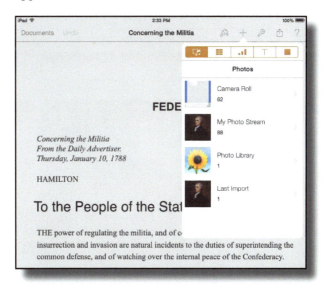

39

Select a source; then tap on the photo you want to add. It is added to the document.

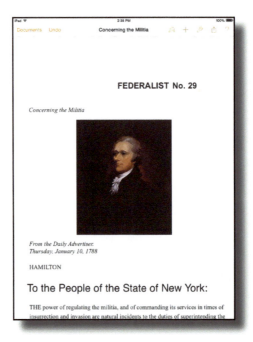

21. Resize and relocate a picture

The photo appears in your document, but it probably not in the size and position you want. You can move and resize it using the positioning handles that appear as blue dots around the border.

If the buttons do
not appear, tap on
the photo to display
them.

Move the photo

Drag the photo to the position you want. If you want to align the photo to a margin, a yellow guideline will help guide you.

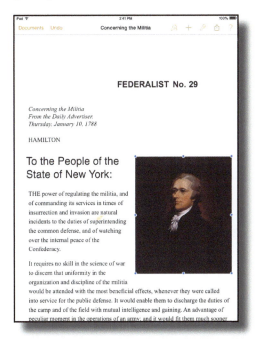

Resize the photo

Move any of the handles to change the picture to the size you want. As you resize the picture, its size and a diagonal indicator appear.

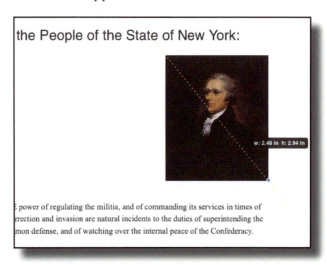

Add styles and borders

Select the picture; then tap on the **Style** button on the toolbar. Pages displays an assortment of suggested border designs.

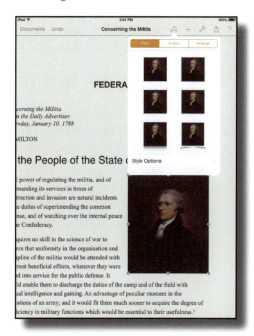

You can tap on any of these to apply it.

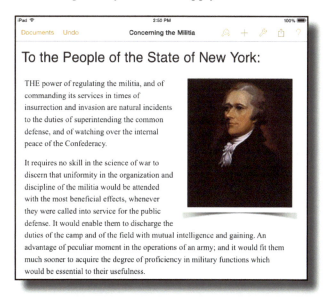

You can expand your range of choices by tapping on **Style Options.**

Select the **Effects** option, and you can apply shadows or reflections, and control their opacity. Turn on the desired type of effect, and you can see the available options.

Select the **Border** option, turn it on, and you can select the color, width, and appearance of a border.

22. Crop the image

You can crop an image to move in on its center to emphasize the main subject. Pages crops an image by placing a mask over the unwanted areas.

Apply the mask

Double-tap on the image. A mask control appears near-by; its exact position depends on its place on the screen.

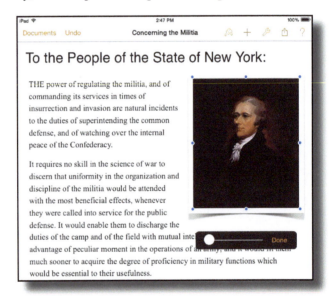

Apply the mask

Slide the control to apply the mask and establish the new boundaries of the image. Drag to the right to enlarge the picture, to the left to make it smaller. You also can move the image within the mask to make the right selection

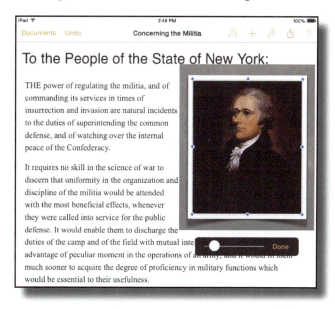

Complete the process

Tap outside the image. The cropped version appears.

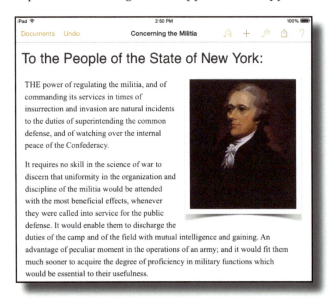

23. Add a text box

You can insert a text box into the document, perhaps to contain a pull quote. The procedure is much the same as inserting a picture.

Display the options

Tap on the **Insert** button in the toolbar. Then tap on the **T** button. You can choose from a variety of text box options.

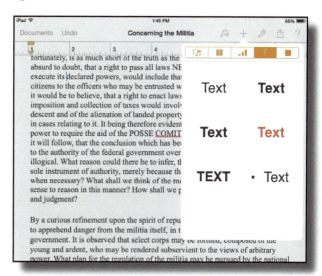

Insert the text box

Tap on the type effect you want. A text box appears in the document. At first, it's probably the wrong size and in the wrong place.

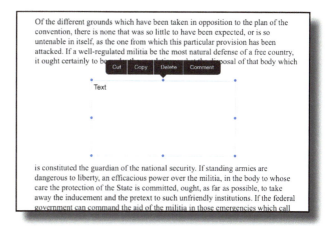

Position and resize the box

Drag the box to the position you want it to appear. Use the sizing handles to set its size and position.

Enter the text.

For more on how to position and dis-play a box, see "24. Customize a box or shape" and "25. Wrap text around a box".

Delete the **Text** label. In its place, type the text you want to use, or paste text copied from another source.

government can command the aid of the militia in those emergencies which call for the military arm in support of the civil magistrate, it can the better dispense with the employment of a different kind of force. If it cannot avail itself of the former, it will be obliged to recur to the latter. To render an army unnecessary, will be a more certain method of preventing its existence than a thousand prohibitions upon paper.

If a well-regulated militia be the most natural defense of a free country, it ought certainly to be under the regulation and at the disposal of that body which is constituted the guardian of the national security.

In order to cast an odium upon the power of calling forth the militia to execute the laws of the Union, it has been remarked that there is nowhere any provision in the proposed Constitution for calling out the POSSE COMITATUS, to assist the magistrate in the execution of his duty, whence it has been inferred, that military force was intended to be his only auxiliary. There is a striking incoherence in the objections which have appeared, and sometimes even from the same quarter, not

Add a shape

You can also add a shape and manipulate it in the same way. Use the **Shape** button at the top of the Insert window.

The main difference is that the shape has no text to edit. It does have colors you can alter; in the shape display, scroll to the right to see them.

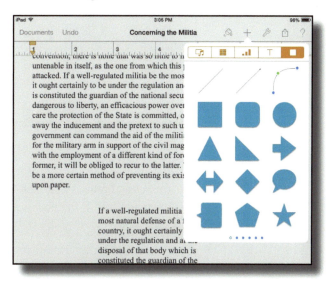

24. Customize a box or shape

For more on styling boxes and shapes, see *"25. Wrap text around a box"*

If you are working with a text box, you can resize the box to better suit its contents. In the same way, you can alter the dimensions of an inserted shape

Restyle selected text

Select the text inside the box.

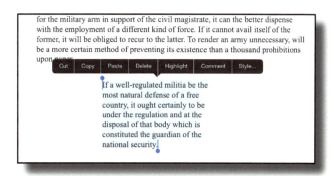

Reminder: Triple-tapping on the text selects an entire paragraph.

Tap on the **Style** icon. You can style the selected text using the same methods you would use to style other text. Apply a distinctive style.

with the employment of a different kind of force. If it cannot avail itself of the former, it will be obliged to recur to the latter. To render an army unnecessary, will be a more certain method of preventing its existence than a thousand prohibitions upon paper.

If a well-regulated militia be the most natural defense of a free country, it ought certainly to be under the regulation and at the disposal of that body which is constituted the guardian of the national security.

In order to cast an odium upon the power of calling forth the militia to execute the laws of the Union, it has been remarked that there is nowhere any provision in the

You can use the Layout section to arrange the boxed text in two or more columns.

Resize the box

Use the sizing handles to adjust the size of the box to the formatted text. If necessary, move the box to a new position.

with the employment of a different kind of force. If it cannot avail itself of the former, it will be obliged to recur to the latter. To render an army unnecessary, will be a more certain method of preventing its existence than a thousand prohibitions upon paper.

If a well-regulated militia be the most natural defense of a free country, it ought certainly to be under the regulation and at the disposal of that body which is constituted the guardian of the national security.

In order to cast an odium upon the power of calling forth the militia to execute the laws of the Union, it has been remarked that there is nowhere any provision in the

25. Wrap text around a box

You can leave the box free-floating, or you can wrap the main text around it.

Select the box

Select the box, and tap on the **Style** button. Select the **Arrange** group.

Pick a wrap

Tap on **Wrap**. A list of text wrapping options opens.

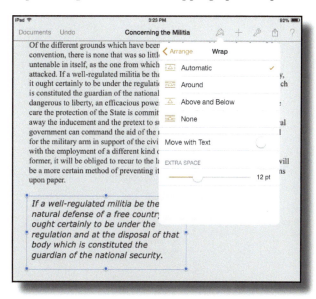

Select an option from the list. If the boxed text is related to a specific part of the main text, you can specify that the text box should move with the surrounding text. You can also improve appearance and readability by adding or subtracting space around the box.

26. Add a chart

Charts and graphs often are effective communication devices, and you can insert them into a Pages document. Once there, you can restyle them and enter data for the chart to display.

Select a chart

Place the insertion point where you want the chart to appear. Tap on the Insert button on the Toolbar. From the window that opens, select the **Charts** symbol.

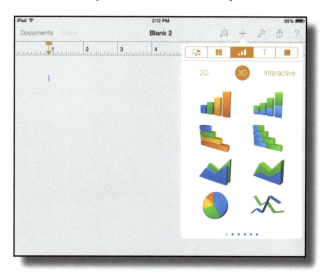

Display either 2D, 3D or Interactive charts, depending on which you'd rather use.

Interactive charts are additional types that allow on-screen adjustments.

Tap on the style you want to use. You can scroll to the right to see a variety of color options. The selected chart type appears in the document.

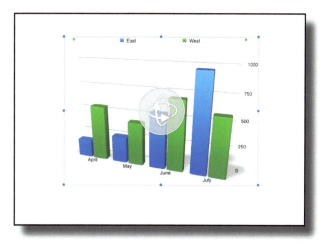

Edit the data

Initially, the suggested chart styles reflect the colors of the template used to create the document. Scroll right to see alternatives.

The chart is initially populated with placeholder data. Tap on **Edit Data** to enter your own figures.

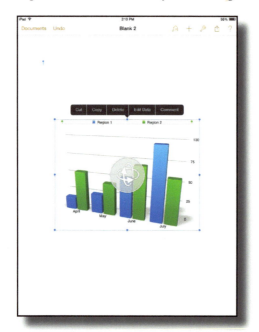

If the menu with this choice does not appear, tap in the middle of the chart.

A table and keyboard allow you to enter your own data.

When you are finished, tap on **Done**. The chart reappears with your data reflected.

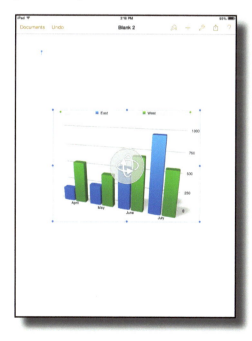

Customize the chart

Select the chart, and tap on the **Style** icon. In the window that opens, tap on **Chart Options**. A variety of options opens for styling and formatting the chart.

These options include:

- Adding a chart title.

- Hiding or displaying the Legend, which explains the chart's structure.

- Selecting a different type face for chart text, and making it larger or smaller.

- Altering the depth of a 3-D chart.

- Changing the shape of chart elements.

- Choosing a different type of charts.

Make your selections; then, tap on **Chart**. The finished chart is displayed.

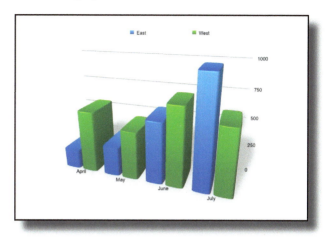

27. Add a table

Tables are also often an effective way to display information. You can add tables in much the same way you can add charts. You then can customize the chart to change its colors, heading rows and columns, type styles, and other characteristics.

Add the table

Tap on the spot where you want the table to appear. Tap on the **Insert** button; then select the **Tables** button. Various combinations of header layouts are presented. You can scroll to the right to see alternative color schemes.

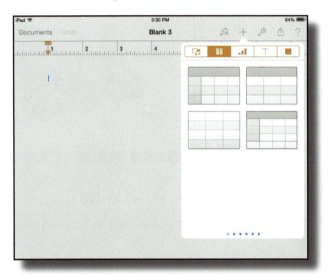

Select the style you want. The table appears in the document.

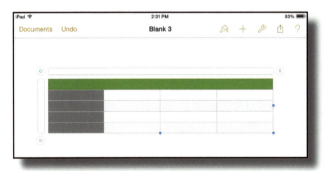

Adjust the number of rows and columns

Symbols at the upper-right and lower-left let you specify the number of columns and rows. Tap on either to
change the current settings to fit your needs. A graphic
shows the current number of rows or columns. Use its
arrows to make changes.

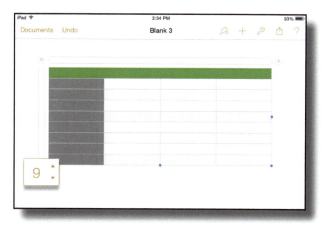

Position the table

If necessary, tap on the table to select it. Blue adjustment
handles appear at the edges of a selected table. Drag the
table to the position you want. Use the handles to adjust
its size.

Format a table

Once the table is in position, you can format the entire
table or selected cells.

To format the entire table, select the table; then tap on
the **Style** icon. Three buttons at the top offer options for
styling the table.

The **Style** button lets you change the table's color scheme and layout.

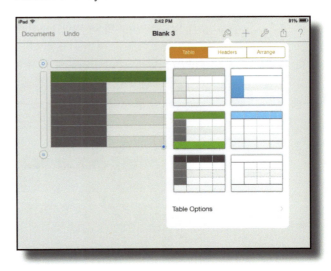

The **Header** button lets you add or subtract header and footer rows.

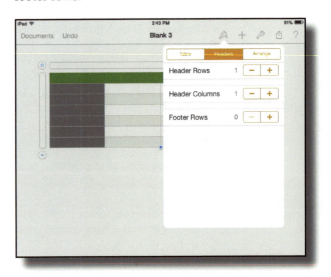

Arrange lets you move the table relative to other graphic elements. You can also wrap adjacent text around it.

Select options

Under the **Table** button, tap on **Table Options**. Select from any of the displayed Options. This applies them to the entire table.

These options include naming the table, giving it a border, and shading alternate rows.

Select specific cells

You also can select any cell or adjacent group of cells for specific formatting. For example, you might want to bold-face the type in the header cells.

Tap on a single cell to select it. You then can use selection handles to extend the selection to adjacent cells.

Tap in the bars at the top and left-hand side of the chart to select an entire row.

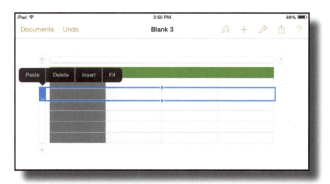

You can also insert data here or delete the selected cells.

Format selected cells

With the cells selected, tap on the **Style** icon. Then, select **Cell**. Use these options to give a distinctive appearance to the selected cells.

For example, you might want to emphasize a particular cell by giving it a distinctive fill color or border.

NUMBERS

Chapter 5. Open a spreadsheet

You probably know what a spreadsheet is: a table filled with data, usually numerical, along with formulas for—presumably—useful calculations. It bears its name because it can easily spread across a huge area. The original spreadsheets were single sheets which did exactly that.

Now a Numbers spreadsheet can contain multiple tables, charts, photos and text spread over several pages in an even greater variety of layouts. You can use these tools to create your own spreadsheet, or you can adapt one of the templates Numbers provides as starting points.

The iPad version of numbers is, of course, closely related to the version that runs on Mac desktops. The two applications basically reflect the differences—both positive and negative—between the iPad and Mac systems.

28. What's on the screen?

Numbers' controls are right at your fingertips—literally. As with other iPad iWork applications, when you display a spreadsheet, you can zoom in or out by pinching the screen. When you are zoomed in, you can pan the display by dragging across the screen.

You have the immediate choice of horizontal (landscape) or vertical (portrait) views. Rotate the iPad, and the display will adapt.

Control your view

A toolbar at the top of the screen contains some basic controls:

- **Spreadsheets**: Opens a display of existing Spreadsheets. Provides for opening a new spreadsheet.

- **Undo**. Reverses the previous action. If you change your mind again, touch and hold to redo the action.

- **Format** (the paintbrush icon). Change the appearance of a selected item.

- **Insert** (the plus sign). Add an element to the spreadsheet.

- **Tools** (the wrench). Print, search, change settings, or display help.

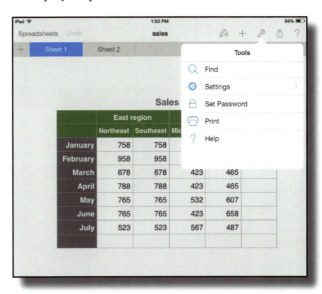

- **Share**. Share your work with others or open the sheet in another application. You have the choice of Numbers, Excel, PDF (Acrobat) or CSV (comma-separated) formats.

- **Help** (the question mark). display tool tips or activate the conventional help file.

29. Start a new spreadsheet

To start a new spreadsheet, you must apply a template. Even if you want to start with a blank piece of paper, you must start with a blank template.

Then, you can go about adding or replacing text and graphics.

Open the Spreadsheets view

If you have no other open spreadsheets at the moment, Numbers should do this for you. Otherwise, tap on on on Spreadsheets in the upper left-hand corner of the screen. You should see a display of your existing spread-sheets.

If you want to open an existing spreadsheet, tap on it. If you want to create a new sheet, tap on **Create Spreadsheet**.

Start the process

In Spreadsheets view, tap on **Create Spreadsheet**. Numbers displays the available templates for new spreadsheets.

Scroll down, if necessary, to find a template that fits the type of spreadsheet you want to create. Tap on on that template, and a new spreadsheet opens with the selected layout.

Enter data

Spreadsheets can have multiple pages. Tabs across the top of the display are attached to other pages.

If you've chosen a blank template, you can start typing right away. Otherwise, you'll undoubtedly notice some content that really doesn't apply. This is placeholder content you can replace with more relevant material of your own.

30. Replace placeholder text

If you're building a spreadsheet from a template, you'll see plenty of things you want to replace. In fact, you could well want to replace everything, and enter your own contents into the template format.

Select the text

To replace placeholder contents, or to enter information in a cell, double-tap on on the placeholder text or in the cell you want to use. To replace heading text that is not in a cell, double-tap to select a word; triple-tap on to select a paragraph. The selected text opens for editing.

Once you've selected text, you also can cut, copy, and paste.

Type the new text

When the keyboard opens, type the text you want to use.

31. Replace placeholder pictures

You also can replace the placeholder pictures with those of your choosing.

Select the picture

In the lower right-hand corner of each placeholder picture is an editing symbol.

Tap on that symbol. Pictures on the iPad are arranged into albums, and a list of these albums opens.

Tap on the album that contains the picture you want to insert. The pictures in that album are displayed.

Tap on the picture you want to include. It is automatically added to the document, replacing the placeholder picture.

Chapter 6. Tables and columns

The heart of every spreadsheet is the table. There also may be charts, illustrations, headings and other elements, but mainly you will see one or more tables, mostly filled with numerical entries and calculations.

If you want to add a table to a sheet, Numbers can start you off with a choice of table layouts in a variety of color schemes. The layouts differ mainly in the number and positions of their headings.

32. Add a table

From the basic layouts, you can pick a table that meets your needs and drag it onto the sheet. From there, you can place the table in position, add or subtract rows and columns, and enter information in the table cells,

Place a table on the sheet

Tap on the **Add** button in the toolbar. In the dialog box that opens, tap on the symbol for **Tables**. A selection of table styles opens.

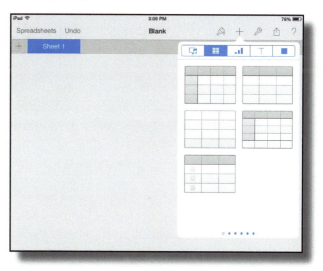

You can scroll to the right to see these tables in varied color schemes.

The available table styles may not be exactly what you need, but there probably is one that comes close. Tap on

75

that one; it appears on the sheet. You can modify it as you go.

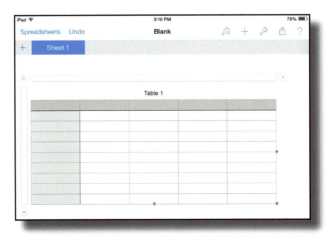

Position the table

When you select the table, handles appear in three of the four corners. Drag the handle in the upper left-hand corner to position the table in the sheet.

You can use this handle later if you want to copy, move, or resize the table. See "33. *Adjust and reposition the table*".

33. Adjust and reposition the table

For information on how to add data to the table, see "34. *Get information into a table*".

Tap on the handle in the upper left-hand corner of the table. Blue resizing handles appear around the edge of the table. Among other things, you can use them to resize the table.

Freeze table headers

It can be annoying when you scroll a large table down or to the right to see the row and column headers slide off the screen. You can freeze these headings so they remain on the screen as you scroll.

Select the table; then, tap on the **Style** button on the Toolbar. Next, tap on **Headers**. You then can specify the number of header rows and columns you want to use.

You can also turn on **Freeze Rows** and **Freeze Columns** as you prefer.

Apply a different color scheme

Perhaps you'd like to apply a different color scheme to your table. If so, select the table; then tap on the **Style** button. Then, tap on **Table**. A selection of different table styles opens with different color schemes.

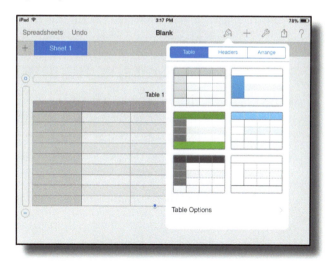

Tap on the style you want to apply; the change appears instantly in the table.

Exercise other options

You can change other elements of the table by tapping **Table Options** at the bottom of the window. In the new window that opens, you can display or hide the table name and border and choose whether to emphasize alternating rows, often an aid to readability.

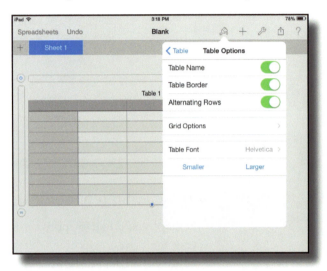

Within the Table Options window, tap on **Grid Options** to specify which lines in the table to highlight. You can also change the text size or typeface.

34. Get information into a table

Numbers tables are made up of rows and columns. The intersection of a row and column is a cell. The cell's coordinates within the table are its address. For example the cell at the intersection of Column B and Row 3 has the address B3.

But then you probably knew that already.

In each cell, you can enter a number, a formula, text data, and much more.

Enter basic information

To make an entry, or to edit data that is already there, double-tap on the cell. A keyboard opens at the bottom of the screen.

Above the keyboard, an **Input Bar** displays the data you are entering.

Symbols to the left of the Input Bar let you select different keyboards for different purposes.

The keyboard layout varies, according to whether you are entering text, numbers, or some other kind of information. Most Numbers choices are different from the standard iPad keyboards.

- The **42** button calls up a keyboard for numeric entries.

- The next button to the right, with an L-shaped symbol, opens a keyboard you can use to enter sequential information like dates or times.

- The **T** button produces a text entry keyboard.

- The = button displays a keyboard for entering mathematical formulas (see "32. *Add a table*").

Move from cell to cell

If you're typing data in more than one cell, you can use a **Next** key to move from cell to cell. In some keyboards, a key with a right-pointing arrow moves you to the next cell to the right. A key with the broken arrow moves you the left-hand side of the next row.

If you tap on the straight-arrow key at the end of a row, the program will add another column. Likewise, if you use the broken-arrow key at the bottom of a column, your table will gain a new row.

35. Merge cells

If you expand your table by accident, see "*33. Adjust and reposition the table*" for how to remove the unwanted addendum.

Sometimes it's useful to merge several cells into one. You may often do this to center a title over several columns.

Start by selecting the cells you want to merge.

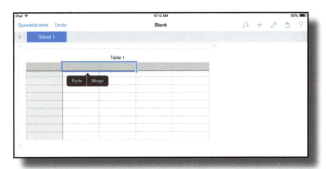

In the menu bar that appears, tap on **Merge**. The selected cells are combined. You then can enter the information you want the cells to contain

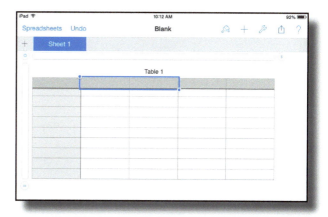

Though merged cells are used most often for headings, there are times when they might contain numbers for calculations. If you want a calculation to refer to a merged cell, specify the address of the cell that forms the upper left-hand corner of the merged cell.

36. Insert rows and columns

Use this upper-left address whenever you want to refer to the whole merged cell. If you try to refer to any other part of the cell, you can mess yourself up seriously.

A Numbers table initially displays a standard number of rows and columns, and the columns are at predetermined widths. Chances are none of these standard dimensions will fit your needs. You may have headings that are winder than the usual columns, and the numbers or rows and columns can range from seriously insufficient to vast excess.

Fortunately, you can readjust all these things.

Add or remove columns or rows

When you select anything within an open table, it displays sizing symbols at the lower left-hand and upper right-hand columns.

To add columns, you can drag the upper-right symbol to the right. Likewise, you can remove columns by dragging it to the left.

To add rows, drag the lower-left symbol downward. To

remove rows, drag it up.

Insert within the table

Also see *"33. Adjust and reposition the table"*.

These methods add and subtract columns from the right-hand side and rows from the bottom. This may or may not work for you, particularly if you want to modify a table that already has some information in it. Should your needs require, you also can add rows and columns within the table.

To add a column in this way, select an existing column.

Then tap on **Insert**. A new column is added to the left of the selected one.

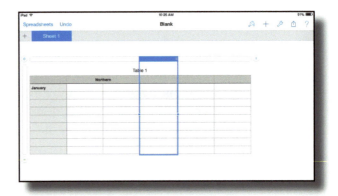

In the same way, you can select a row and tap on Insert to add a row above.

Delete rows or columns

Reminder: Select a row or column by tapping on the gray bar above or to the left.

This is simple: select the row or column; then, tap on **Delete**. You can select a range or rows or columns by selecting them all before you tap on **Delete**.

Move rows or columns around

You may decide you want to display rows or columns in a different order. To do that, select the row of column you want to move.

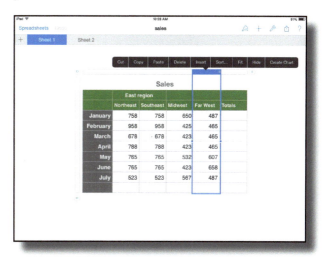

Then, drag it into its new position.

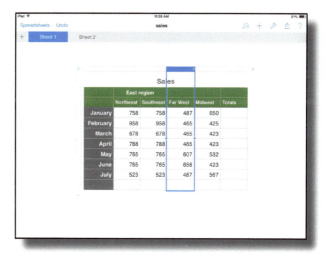

Resize rows and columns

Select the column; then drag the right-hand edge of the blue bar above the selection. You can make the column wider or narrower as you drag.

If you'd rather, you can size a column to precisely fit its contents. Select the column; then tap on Fit. The selected column adjusts its width to the fit the longest entry.

37. Keep your sheets untangled

Left unchecked, a spreadsheet can live up to its name and strew information across vast row-and-column acre-age. Early spreadsheets gave you no choice, but more modern designs, including Numbers, let you consolidate your wide-ranging information on individual pages. Or as Numbers calls them, *sheets*.

Suppose you are a retailer who wants to check out the financial positions of several stores. Each store's profit and loss statement could be entered on a separate sheet. Then you could use a summary sheet to consolidate and analyze the group's overall performance.

Or, you could track your bank accounts with a separate sheet for each account, again with a summary sheet to show your overall balance.

Each sheet is represented by a tab at the top of the display. With these tabs you can:

- Display a different sheet by tapping on its tab.

- Add a new sheet by tapping on the tab that displays a plus sign.

- Rename a sheet by double-tapping on its tab, then typing a new name.

- Change the sheets' order by dragging their tags into new positions.

- Delete or duplicate a sheet by tapping twice on its tab. You then have the option of expanding or contracting.

Chapter 7. Figuring things out

"Figures lie and liars figure," someone once said. Benjamin Disraeli, British prime minister in the Victorian era, invoked a hierarchy of "lies, damned lies, and statistics." No, Mark Twain didn't say that.

But spreadsheets are all about figures and statistics. It's definitely in your interest to make sure that the figures in your spreadsheets don't lie.

First, of course, you must get some information into your table cells. Double-tap on the cell where you want to make the entry. A keyboard appears along with an **Input Bar.**

At the left of the Input Bar are four buttons you can use to determine the type of entry you want to make. You can select a specialized keyboard to enter numbers, dates or times, text, and mathematical formulas.

These keyboards are illustrated and described in *"34. Get information into a table"*.

38. Fill in a series

Lots of times, the data you want to enter will be in a logical series like A to Z or the days of the week. If you give Numbers a good start, it will automatically complete the series.

Start by double-tapping on the cell where you want to start the series. The Input Bar opens. Use it to type the first entry in the series.

When you're ready, tap on **Done**. Tap again on the cell where you made the first entry; then tap on **Fill**. A yellow box surrounds the cell.

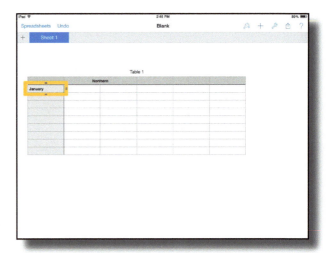

Drag the box to include the cells where you want to complete the series. Numbers figures out what you are trying to do and completes the entries.

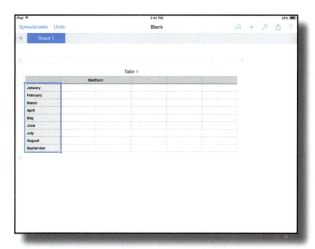

39. Add a column of figures

Chances are, one of your most frequent activities is to total a column of figures. The **SUM** function shortcuts this process.

Double-tap on an empty cell where you want the results to appear. SUM anticipates that you'll select a cell at the bottom of a column of figures. Then tap on the = sign in the Input Bar. The keyboard that opens includes a **Sum** key.

Tap on it. As you might expect, the program totals the amounts in the cells above it.

40. Total a selected range

If this isn't the range you want to total, you can select the range of your choosing. Perhaps you want to total a row instead of a column.

Double-tap on the cell where you want the results to appear. Tap on =, then the **SUM** key. Then, select the range of cells you want to total.

Be careful not to include the results cell in the range.

Tap on the green check mark at the end of the Input Bar. The total of the selected cells is displayed.

41. Copy formulas to other cells

Often, you will want to total a row of columns or a column of rows, as strange as that may sound. You can total the values in one row or column, then copy the formula to the other rows or columns in the table.

For instance, you can total the sales figures in one column, then copy the SUM formula to other cells to total the sales in their columns.

Select the source

Total the amounts in one column or row. Tap on the cell where this total appears; then tap on Copy.

Select the range

Now, select the range to which you want to copy the formula.

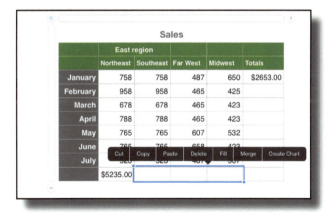

Then, tap on **Paste**. A new menu gives you the option of pasting the value in the source cell or the formula. Choose **Paste Formulas**.

These options are plural because you can also copy from a range of cells.

The results appear in the selected cells. You also can use the same method to copy the formula used to total selected rows.

42. Freeze cell addresses in calculations

Calculations such as those in *"40. Total a selected range"* use relative references to cells a certain distance and direction from the cell where the results are displayed. In that way, a formula copied to another column can sum the figures in the new column.

That's often the result you want, but occasionally you

want a fixed reference where the copied formula always refers to the value in the original cell.

For example, you might want to calculate the sales totals for each of several regions as a percentage of overall sales. If so, you will want to freeze the cell address that contains the overall sales total when you copy the formula to each region's column.

Start the calculation

Double-tap on the cell where you want the first region's percentage to appear.

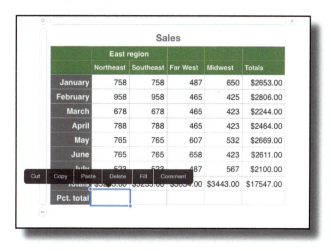

Enter the formula

In the Input Bar, tap on =. Enter the formula to calculate the percentage. In this case, it is the region's sales divided by total sales. Don't complete the calculation just yet.

In the Input Bar, tap on the up arrow for the cell whose address you want to freeze. If you've selected a range, a menu lets you freeze the addresses that appear at the start or end of that range. If you've selected a single cell, that cell is at both ends of the range.

Back in the Input Bar, tap on the green check mark to complete the calculation.

Copy the formula to the cells that represent the percentages for the other regions. Each displays that region's sales totals as a fraction of the overall total.

Initially, these cells may display fractions instead of percentages. You can change this by selecting the cells, then tapping on the Style button. Under **Cells**, tap on **Percentage**.

You also can change the number of decimal points displayed. Select the percentage cells; then tap on the **Style** paintbrush.

Tap on the **i** symbol to the right of **Percentage**. Use the arrows after **Decimal** to set the number of places.

43. Insert functions into cells

Numbers has an ape's-arm list of mathematical functions you can use in your calculations. Need to compute something advanced like a standard deviation? You can do that easily—well, fairly easily— with the SDEV function.

SUM is the most commonly used function; so common it has its own key on the keyboard used to enter mathematical formulas. To use other functions, double-tap on the cell where you want the result to appear. Tap on =. Then tap on the **Functions** key. It opens up a vast array of possibilities. You can choose from a list of recently-used functions or display the full array organized into categories. You can scroll down to see all the available categories.

For example, if you want to compute the average of several cells, select **Average**. Then select the range of cells you want to average.

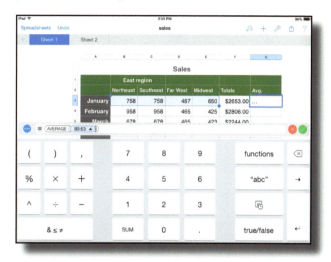

Tap on the green check mark at the end of the Input Bar. The calculated average appears in the target cell.

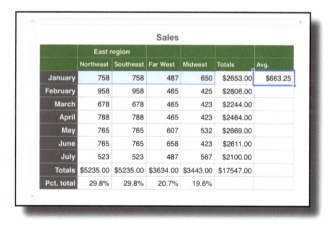

44. Sort a column of data

You can sort the data in a column to display it in alphabetical or numeric order. And you can sort either forward or backward.

Start by tapping on the bar above the column you want to sort. The entire column is selected and a menu of options is displayed.

Tap on **Sort**. You are given the choice of sorting in ascending or descending order. The table is sorted as you directed.

Headers are not included in the sort.

45. Chart your data

A spreadsheet need not be a static piece of rows, columns, and numbers. Charts, graphics, and other visual aids can improve communication by showing trends and differences, and by calling attention to the most salient information.

A chart is a useful way to identify trends and emphasize key information. Numbers gives you the means to display a variety of chart types in an equal variety of color schemes. There are two main ways to do this. You can create a chart and then add data, or you can do the reverse: select a range of data and create a chart that displays it.

Apply data to a chart

Select the range of data you want to display in the chart.

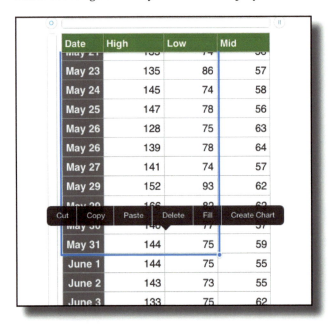

Tap on the **Create Chart**. An array of chart designs appears. You have a choice of 2D, 3D or Interactive charts.

Interactive charts are additional types that allow on-screen adjustments.

The initial chart selection displays colors appropriate to your selected template. Scroll to the right to see alternatives.

Select the type of chart you want, and drag it into position on the spreadsheet page.

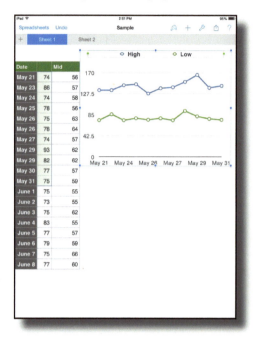

You can move and resize the chart, using the blue handles. Double-tap the title to enter your own. Tap outside the chart to hide the controls.

46. Control the range of cell entries.

If you selected a 3-D chart, a circular graphic appears in front of the chart. You can use it to adjust the angle at which the chart appears.

If someone enters an inaccurate value into a cell, the results can range from comical to catastrophic. Numbers gives you several ways to ensure that entries are within a certain range or conform to a list of acceptable values. One way is to add a slider, a movable button that inserts a chosen value from within an acceptable range.

Select the cells to be affected.

You can apply the slider to a single cell or to a range of cells. Start by selecting the cell or cells. Then tap on the **Style** button and **Format**. A list of formatting options is displayed.

Set minimum and maximum values

From this list, select **Slider**. Tap on the **i** at the right-hand end of the button. Options for setting the slider are displayed.

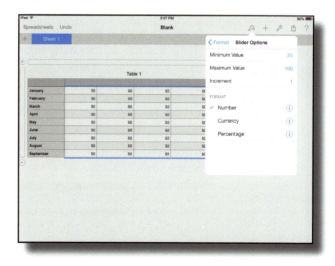

Here, you can set minimum and maximum values for

the slider scale and the interval between values within that range. You can also choose whether to display the cell contents as numbers, currency, or percentages.

Enter the values you want to use. Then tap the affected cell. A slider appears next to it. You can move this slider to display the value you want to use.

Table 1					
January	50	50	50	50	36
February	50	50	50	50	62
March	50	50	50	50	50
April	50	50	50	50	74
May	50	50	50	50	50
June	50	50	50	50	50
July	50	50	50	50	50
August	50	50	50	50	50
September	50	50	50	50	50

47. Restrict entries to a list

A similar feature called a stepper replaces the slider with a pair of arrows you can use to click to choose between designated values.

There also are times when you'd like to make sure entries are restricted to items on a particular list. You've probably seen on-line forms that ask you to enter a state. To prevent you from typing something like *Califunria* or *Michigang,* you are asked to select from a list of the 50 states. You can also make your life easily by forcing users to select from a list of state abbreviations rather than the fully-spelled-out names.

Numbers provides for pop-up menus that do the same thing. You can add them by tapping on the **Format** button, then selecting **Format** again. Select **Pop-Up Menu**. The options for this feature are displayed.

In each item block, type one of the items you want to appear in the list. If you want a list of more than three items—as you will if you are entering the names of 50 states—you can tap add new item to expand the display. Your list can hold as many as 100 items.

You also can choose whether the cell will initially display the first object on the list or will be blank.

Tap on the cell, and the list will appear next to it. Then, tap the item you want to appear.

Chapter 8. Solve financial problems

In the Popeye comic strip, the character of Wimpy was famous for saying, "I would gladly pay you Thursday for a hamburger today." In statistical terms, Wimpy was asking you to assess the future value of today's cost of the hamburger.

Numbers is not just about adding and subtracting. Its advanced tools give you the means to solve problems much more complex than Wimpy's freeloading.

This chapter focuses on using Numbers' financial functions to improve your ability to decide whether to be a lender or borrower. It will also help you understand how Numbers functions give you the mathematical ability to solve even complex problems.

48. Give me an argument

To enter a function, double-tap on the cell where you want the function's results to appear. When the Input Bar opens, tap the = button. Then tap on the **Functions** key and select the function you want to use.

The function will appear in the Input Bar along with an array of *arguments*. These call for the numeric data the function must have to do its work.

Tap on each of these arguments. Then, enter a value or select one or more cells that contain the needed information. The selections are color-coded to match the displayed arguments. When you're through, tap on the green check mark. The result should appear in the selected cell.

49. Match actions with results

Does more spending for advertising lead to an increase in sales? And if so, is it by an amount that justifies the added expense? You can match up the advertising expenses with the sales results and see how well they match up.

Set up the relationship

A statistical tool that does this is called the coefficient of correlation. That's heavy language for a Numbers function that determines how well two sets of numbers relate to each other.

In Numbers, this function is called CORREL. It compares the two sets of numbers to see how closely changes in one set produce changes in the other. This function returns results ranging between 1 and -1. These values mean:

- **1** means the two groups of data have a direct and positive relationship. For every change in the first set there is an equal change in the second set. For example, it would mean that if you increased your advertising budget by 10 percent, sales also went up 10 percent.

- **Between 0 and 1** means the data sets have a positive relationship but not a perfect one. The larger the result the stronger the relationship is.

- **0** means the two groups have no relationship at all. In other words, the amount you spend on advertising has absolutely no effect on sales.

- **Between 0 and -1** means the two groups have a negative relationship. Such a result would indicate that more advertising actually decreases sales.

- **-1** means a perfect negative correlation. A 10 percent increase in advertising would cause a 10 percent decrease in sales.

Set up the data

To assess the effects of your advertising, set up a column that lists your advertising expenses over several months. In another column, enter the sales results for the same months.

Pick the function

Select the **CORREL** function; it's in the **Statistical** group.

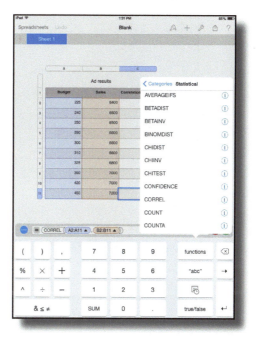

The Input Bar displays prompts for two arguments. Compared with many functions, these are fairly simple.

Tap on **y-values**; then select the first range of values. In this case, it would be the column of advertising expenses. Then tap x-values and select the other range, in this case the sales results. Tap on the green check mark, and the results appear in the selected cell. In this case, the rounded-off result of 0.98 is a strong indicator that increased advertising produces increased sales.

This result may appear with a huge number of decimal places. You can reduce these by selecting the cell and tapping **Format** > **Format** (again). Now tap the **i** symbol after **Numbers**. You then can reduce the number of decimal places to a more useful span.

50. Figure the payments on a loan

That new car looks awfully nice, but can you afford the payments? The PMT function will calculate them for you. In the worksheet, enter the amount you want to finance, the interest rate, and the number of monthly payments. A couple of optional arguments call for a future value of the car and whether payments are due at the beginning or end of the month. You are free to ignore these.

The function's arguments include the interest rate, the length of the loan, and the amount borrowed.

Make sure the interest rate and number of payments use the same time periods. You can enter the length of the loan in months, and in the completed formula you can divide the annual interest rate by 12.

Since the payments are outflows from your checking account or other resources, the result appears as a negative amount.

Other uses

You can also use this procedure to calculate the return on an investment. In this case, enter the amount of the investment as a negative figure, since it is an amount you pay out. The return is a positive figure, representing income.

51. Appreciate depreciation

Business assets have specific useful lives. For example ,
a restaurant that installs a new commercial oven might
expect it to last 10 years. It usually cannot deduct the
entire price of the oven on a single year's tax return. It
must depreciate the oven, spreading its cost over the
entire 10-year period.

Depreciation functions can help the business determine
its depreciation during any year of the 10-year span.
There are several ways to figure it (legally), and Numbers has functions to represent each of them:

- **DB**. This function calculates a fixed declining balance
  that lets you compute the allowable depreciation in
  any year of the asset's useful life.

- **DDB**. You're probably familiar with the adage that
  a new car loses a big chunk of its value the moment
  you drive it off the lot. This function acknowledges
  that many assets lose value more rapidly in the early
  stages of their lives.

- **SLN**. This function calculates straight-line depreciation, assuming that the asset loses value at a uniform
  rate throughout its life.

- **SYD**. Sum-of-the-year's digits. This is an accelerated
  depreciation function with which you can determine
  the depreciation over a particular time period.

- **VDB**. Variable declining balance. This function calculates the depreciation over any time span you specify.

These are similar functions, and they take various combinations of similar arguments. These include:

- **Cost**, the initial cost of the asset.

- **Life**, the number of time periods over which to depreciate the asset. This usually is expressed in years, but
  it could be any kind of repeatable time period.

- **Depr-Period**, the particular year or other time period

for which you want to calculate the depreciation.

- **Depr-Factor**, the rate at which depreciation is acceler-ated relative to straight-line depreciation. Unless you change it, its value is set at 2.

- **Salvage**, the asset's value at the end of the deprecia-tion process.

Find the first-year depreciation

It might be easier tho think of this as a trade-in value.

Say you've just agreed to finance $15,000 for a new truck. You expect it to last 10 years, at the end of which it will be worth only $250. Since most of that value will be lost early in its life, you select the DDB depreciation method.

With this knowledge, you can set up a spreadsheet table that computes the depreciation for the first five years

Select the cell where you want to display the first-year depreciation. Activate the DDB function; then select the cells that contain the values for the cost, life, and salvage value. For depr-period enter 1. This formula will compute the first-year depreciation.

For subsequent years, you can use the same formula, changing only the depreciation period.

52. Figure the return on an investment

Using absolute references for the first three items, you can copy the formula to subsequent cells (see *"41. Copy formulas to other cells"*); then open each instance and change the depreciation period.

Congratulations. You've won the lottery. The state offers you two options: you can take your winnings in a lump sum of $1 million or in 20 annual payments of $50,000 each. Which is the better deal?

Numbers has three financial functions that can help you decide between alternatives like this:

- **PV**, present value. This function is designed to look at an investment that returns a series of equal payments. It calculates the present value of these payments.

- **NPV**, Net Present Value. This is similar to **PV**, but it allows for irregular repayments.

- **FV**, Future Value. This function calculates the value of an investment at some future date.

These functions use several common arguments:

- **Future value**, the value of the investment at the end of its term.

- **Present value**, the value of the investment today.

- **Inflows**, periodic payments that differ in their amounts.

- **Payment**, the amount of each payment when the payments are equal.

- **Number of periods**, the term of the investment, typically expressed in months.

- **Type**, whether the payment is made at the beginning or end of each period.

- **Period**, the number of an individual payment. For example, if the payment is made in the fourth month of the loan term, the Period would be 4.

- **Rate**, the return on an alternative investment. Also called the hurdle rate, this is typically the rate you want your investment to exceed.

Assess the lottery

In the case of the lottery, use the PV function to assess the future value of the payment plan so you can compare it with the lump payout. The option that has the higher future value would be the better choice. The formula looks like this:

113

The payments are calculated to have a present value of nearly $1.8 million, substantially more than the lump sum.

This analysis ignores taxes or the return you could gain from investing the lump sum.

KEYNOTE

Chapter 9. Build a presentation

You've probably endured presentations you would rather miss: the screen is overfilled with static text that the presenter reads verbatim while the same screen stays eternally on display.

Keynote, in both its Mac and iPad versions, can help everyone avoid that experience. Keynote offers a variety of *themes*, model designs you can use to assemble effective combinations of text and artwork. Within each theme is a collection of slide templates you can uses to assemble the right combinations of words and pictures, Then you can add transitions and other graphic effects to help hold the audience's interest.

The iPad edition has fewer combinations of themes and themes than its Mac equivalent.

Once you've built a presentation, you can show it on your iPhone, iPad or iPod Touch or route it to an attached display screen or projector. You can advance the presentation manually or automatically, or you can let the user take control. In the viewer-run mode, you can create a presentation that shows selected slides, depending on the viewer's choices. For example, the presentation could show different screens depending on which button the viewer taps.

You can create the presentation on the iPad. If you prefer, though, you can create the presentation on the Mac version of Keynote; then import it into the iPad.

53. Open an existing presentation

If you previously closed Keynote with an open presentation, that presentation is displayed again when you open the program. If you want to work with a different presentation, tap **Presentations** in the upper left-hand corner.

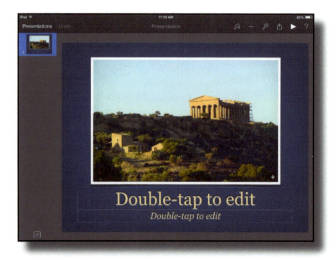

All available presentations are displayed.

Tap on the presentation you want to use; it will open immediately.

54. Build a new presentation

To start a new presentation you must work from a *theme*. Each theme includes one or more *templates* for pages in your presentations. Even if you want to start with a blank sheet, you must use a blank theme. Then you can go about the business of adding text and graphics.

Select a theme

From the Presentations display, tap on the **Create Presentation** window in the upper left-hand corner of the screen. This opens a display of themes and templates.

Scroll down if necessary to find a theme that fits the type of presentation you want to create. Tap on that theme. A new presentation opens with the selected layout.

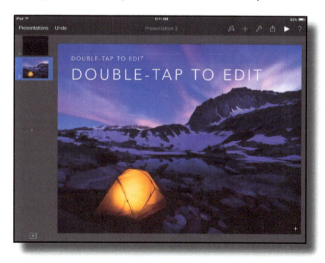

In selecting a theme, look for a suitable layout; ignore the subject matter.

55. Add a slide

Presentations are basically ordered sequences of pages or *slides*. A typical theme includes templates that start with the title slide from that theme. It's up to you to add additional slides. Each theme has an array of slide page templates that provide for various combinations of text and graphics. You can insert the page templates that best match your needs. That slide will display *placeholder* text and graphics. You can replace these with your own content (see *"56. Replace placeholder text"* and *"57. Replace placeholder pictures"*).

Display the slides

Tap on the **Plus** symbol in the lower left-hand corner of the display. Thumbnail views of the page templates in your chosen theme are displayed on the left-hand side of the display.

Select a thumbnail; then tap on it. A new page with that layout is added to the presentation.

56. Replace placeholder text

If you're building a document from a theme, you'll see plenty of things you want to replace.

First, undoubtedly, is the text that reads, "Double-tap to edit." That's exactly what you should do, since you probably want something that's actually appropriate to your subject. The process of adding your text is ridiculously simple.

Add new text

As instructed, double-tap on the text you want to replace. The old text disappears, and a keyboard and insertion point are displayed.

Type the new text

Type the text you want to add. That's it. Your new text appears in the document.

57. Replace placeholder pictures

You also can replace the placeholder pictures with those of your choosing.

Select the picture

In the lower right-hand corner of each placeholder picture is an editing symbol.

Tap on that symbol. Pictures on the iPad are arranged into albums, and a list of these albums opens.

Tap on the album that contains the picture you want to insert. The pictures in that album are displayed.

Tap on the picture you want to include. It is automatically added to the document, replacing the placeholder picture.

Adjust the picture

Chances are, the picture you chose and the picture you replaced are not exactly the same size and shape. For example, if the new picture is proportionately wider than the original, the opening that held the original photo will mask the outer edges.

Double-tap on the image. Its full dimensions become visible through the mask.

A mask slider above or below the picture lets you enlarge or reduce the displayed image. Slide right to enlarge the picture, left to make it smaller. You also can use the adjustment buttons around its edges to fit the picture as you desire. Make the adjustments you want; then tap anywhere outside the picture. The picture appears in its new size and position.

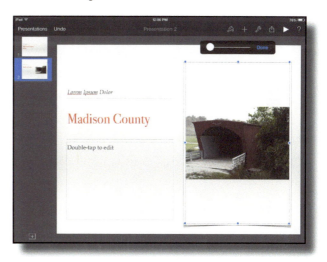

58. Keep your presentation in order

At first, your slides are arranged in the order in which you added them. Thumbnail images are displayed in the *Slide Navigator* on the left-hand edge of the screen.

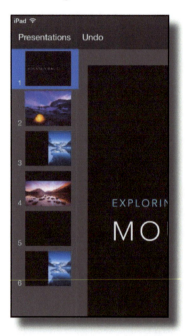

The order in which you created these slides may not be the order in which you want to present them. In that event, you can move slides to change the order, whether it's one slide or a large group.

Move a slide

You can use the Slide Navigator to move a slide to a different position in the order. Touch and hold the slide's thumbnail. It will grow an expanded border, and you can move it around.

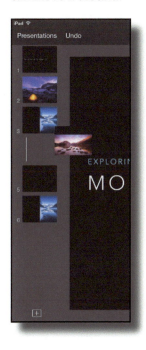

Drag the slide to its new position in the order.

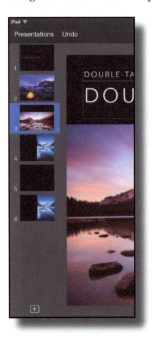

Duplicate a slide

You may want to use more than one slide that applies
the same basic layout but with some minor differences.
Once you've completed one of these slides, you can
duplicate it. You then can make the needed changes
without having to start from scratch.

Slowly double-tap the slide you want to duplicate. From the menu that appears, tap on **Copy**.

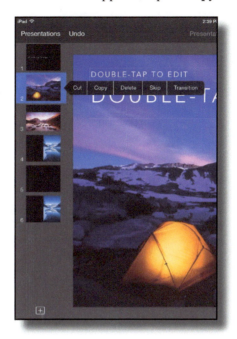

Then, tap the thumbnail for the slide you want the selected slide to appear *after*.

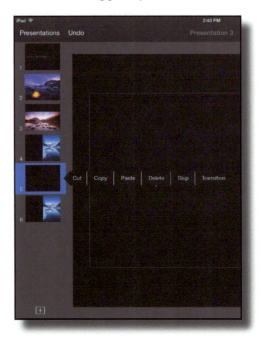

Tap on **Paste**. The duplicated slide appears in the new position.

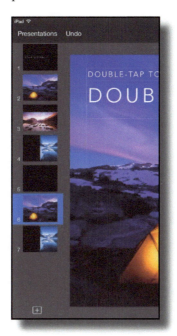

You can use the same double-tap selection procedure to delete the slide, skip it in the presentation, or select transition effects. See *"65. Make more interesting transitions"*.

This requires two hands, even for non-beginners.

59. Select multiple slides

To manage more than one slide at a time, you can select them as a set. Then you can move, copy, delete, or skip them all at once.

Touch and hold the thumbnail of one slide. Then tap on the slides you also want to select. They don't have to be consecutive or in any particular order. When you complete the process, the selected slides are grouped into a

set, and a menu allows you to copy, delete, or skip all the
slides in the set.

Chapter 10. Add images, shapes, and text

Keynote templates provide a host of text and graphic placeholders where you can replace the placeholder contents with something of your own choice See *"62. Select and edit text"* and *"60. Add a photo or movie"*.

You aren't limited, though, to those preplanned placements. You can put text and graphics anywhere you'd like. You can even add movies.

60. Add a photo or movie

You can add any picture or movie stored on your iPad; the Photos app stores these items in *albums.*

Select the picture

Display the slide to which you want to add the picture. Tap on the **Plus** sign in the lower right-hand corner. A selection of your available photo albums is displayed.

Pick the album that contains the picture you want to use.

If you are looking for a movie, it will appear in one of the albums. Inserting it is pretty much the same as inserting a still photo.

The pictures in that album are displayed.

Tap on the picture you want to insert. It appears in the slide.

Resize and reposition the picture

The picture probably is not the size or position you want to display. It will take some resizing and adjustment.

The adjustment handles around the picture are there for just that purpose. Use them to resize the picture. Tap on the picture itself to drag it to a new position.

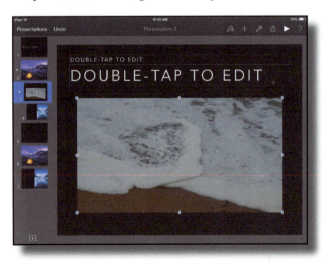

61. Insert a text box

In the world of iWork, a text box is treated as a shape. When you Tap on the **Plus** sign, a text box is one of the options. It appears as a capital **T**.

Tap on the **T**. Sample text boxes are displayed. Tap on your chosen layout; a box with that styling appears on the screen. You can move it to the place you want and use the adjustment handles to set its width.

Initially, the box contains the single word **Text**. Chances are, that's not what you had in mind. Tap on **Text**. That word disappears and is replaced with an insert marker. Type your own text.

Style the box

With the text box selected, Tap on the **Style** button. Tap on **Style** again. Then, tap on **Style Options**. An assortment of fill, effects and border options is displayed.

Tap on the option you'd like. The border and text color appear on the slide.

Style the text

With the text box selected, tap **Style** and then **Text**. A window displays options for setting the type face, size, color, and alignment of the text within the box. You can select a paragraph style, or you can enter your own specifications.

The top element lists the current type face and size. Tap on it, and you can pick your own size, color, and font. You can tap on the arrows in the **Size** block to increase or decrease it.

62. Select and edit text

Text management isn't the iPad's strong point. This is particularly obvious when you want to select a few letters or words. A stylus helps some, but otherwise you must use a cruder instrument—your finger—to make a selection or to select a range of text.

Place the cursor

When the text is small, it helps to use the reverse pinching motion to zoom in on the display.

You can place the cursor or *insertion point* within a block of type, but it isn't necessarily easy.

The basic technique is to tap at the point where you want the insertion point to appear. Chances are, this approach didn't place the bar exactly where you wanted. You have to move it around some. To do this, place your finger on the line of text near the insertion point; you don't have to be precise right now. Hold it until a magnifying glass appears.

137

Now, slide your finger along the line of text, using the magnifier as a guide. When you reach the desired spot, lift your finger. The insertion point should be right where you want it. The operative term is *should be*. Particularly when you're getting started, it will probably take more than one try.

Select phrases and sentences

The easiest way to select a word is to double-tap on it. This is roughly the same thing as double-clicking with a mouse. In the same vein, triple-tapping selects a paragraph.

But what if you want to select a phrase or a sentence? To do that requires a more gentle touch.

When you make a text selection, handles called drag points appear at either side.

True to their name, you can drag these points to incorporate the full range you want to select. As it does with placing an insertion point, a magnifier helps you get to the right spot.

Do something with your selection

If you've gone through the process of selecting text, you've undoubtedly done it for a good reason. Often, you'd like to cut or copy it and paste it somewhere else. A pop-up menu gives you the **Cut** or **Copy** options. Tap on your choice.

Then place the insertion point where you now want the text to appear. Or, if there's text you want to replace, select it. This time, the pop-up menu gives you a **Paste** option.

If you have selected a word, an arrow on the pop-up menu leads to other options. You can look for a list of synonyms for the word or can display a definition.

63. Create a numbered list

The Style option on the pop-up menu does not do what you might expect. It allows you to copy the style of the selected text so you can apply it somewhere else. You can't use it the other way around: to apply a different style to the selection.

A few slide templates provide for preformatted numbered or bulleted lists. They come with placeholder text you can replace. If none of these is available, you can set up a text box and create your own list.

Start the list

Set up a text box to hold the list (see *"61. Insert a text box"*.

Type the first item in the list.

Apply the numbering

Keep the insertion point in the text. Tap on the **Style** button; then tap **List.** The window displays an array of list numbering options, including numbers, letters, ans bullets.. Tap on the style you want to apply. It is applied to the first item.

To display each item separately, see "67. *Build a list item by item*".

Tap on **Return**. The next line continues the numbering sequence.

Continue the list. The numbering sequence is applied automatically.

As a general convention, numbers are used for a list that should be followed in order; bullet points when the order isn't important.

Change the numbering style

Perhaps you have second thoughts and would like to apply a different numbering style. The process is about the same as establishing the style in the first place.

This is different than selecting the text box.

Select the text you want to change.

Tap **Style,** then **List**. Select the new style you'd like to apply.

64. Link with the outside world

Your presentation can include text passages that are linked to web addresses. Then, anyone who is playing the presentation can tap on that passage. The specified web page will open in Safari.

At its most basic, Keynote recognizes these links and automatically turns them into active links. It also applies distinctive formatting. You can tap any of these links immediately and be directed to its connected web site or mailbox.

When you enter a web or e-mail address into your text, Keynote recognizes it and applies distinctive formatting. But maybe you don't want it to work that way. For example, you might want to change *www.apple.com* to *The Apple web site* and still keep the text passage as an active hyperlink. Or, you might want to correct a mistake you made typing the link.

Edit the text

If you want to display something other than the formal web or email address, you can use **Link Settings**. Tap on that option; then tap on **Display**. Type the text you'd rather see. It will continue to be an active hyperlink to the web or email address.

Correct errors

Suppose you entered the hyperlink incorrectly. Because it's an active link, you can't just tap on it and make the correction.

But you can use **Link Settings**. Tap and hold on the link. In the menu that opens, tap on the **Link** entry. The iPad keyboard appears, and you can make any necessary corrections.

You can also use **Link Settings** to remove a link. Tapping that option converts the link to plain text.

65. Make more interesting

transitions

If you do nothing else, your presentation will march slide by slide in routine, unexciting fashion. You can make it easier for your audience to stay awake by inserting animated transitions between slides.

Select the slide

Tap on the thumbnail for the slide to which you want to apply the transition.

From the menu that opens, tap on **Transition**. A new window offers you an extended variety of transition effects.

Select the transition you want to use. Then, tap on **Options** to set further details.

Drag the **Duration** slider at the top of the window to extend or shorten the speed of the transition. If the transition is directional, drag the arrow to set the direction.

66. Move elements between slides

The *Magic Move* feature looks for differences between two adjacent slides and animates the differences. For example, you can move a picture from the first slide to the second, and display it in a different size and position.

Then you can use Magic Move to animate the transition between the first slide and the second. The transition will start with the object as it appears on the first slide. Then, it will slide into its size and position on the second.

An easy way to start a magic move is to select the slide you want to begin the sequence and create a duplicate of it. Then, rearrange the elements of the duplicate to their places on the second slide.

Set up the first slide

Select a slide with the pictures and text elements you want to begin with. If you have such a slide, you can select it. Otherwise, you can edit an existing slide or create a new one.

Make the duplicate

Tap on the first slide; then, tap on **Transition**.

Tap on **Magic Move.** You'll be asked whether you want to duplicate the slide. Select **Yes**.

The duplicate slide is generated.

Edit the duplicate.

Add, delete, resize or rearrange the elements on the copy to the display you want at the end of the transition.

Set options

Stars at the top of the pictures indicate items that will be involved in the transition.

Select the first slide again. Tap on **Magic Move**. Then, tap on **Options** to set further details.

Drag the slider at the top of the window to extend or shorten the speed of the transition.

If you plan a manual presentation, select **On Tap**. With this selection, the transition begins when you Tap on the slide.

For a self-running presentation, select **After Previous Transition**.

Drag the slider at the top of the window to extend or shorten the speed of the transition. If the transition is directional, drag the arrow to set the direction.

When you're finished, tap on **Done** in the upper right-hand corner of the screen.

During this process, you can tap on **Play** in the Transitions heading to see a sample of the transition.

67. Build a list item by item

Any item on a slide—text block, chart, table, shape or picture—can be animated. You can make a graphic spin onto or off the page or display bulleted list one point at a time

This type of animation is called a *build*. A build can either of two basic effects. It can make the object appear on the screen, or you can make it disappear. A variety of build effects provides different ways to implement those two basic motions.

Select the object

Tap on the object you want to use. Then, tap on **Animate**.

A two-headed button appears next to the selected object.

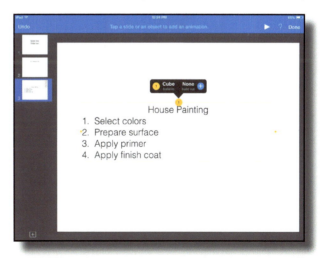

Apply an effect

If an effect has already been applied to this object, its name will appear on the button. Otherwise, the button will bear the label **None**.

Tap on the left-hand button to apply a build-in effect in which the item is animated as it appears on the screen. Tap on the right-hand button to make the item disappear.

A choice of effects is displayed.

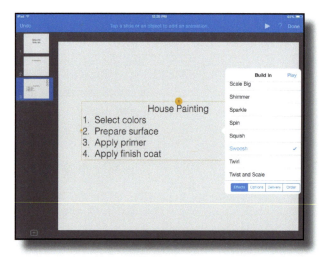

Scroll down to display the full assortment of effects. Tap on the one you prefer. Tap on **Play** to display a preview of the effect.

Set the speed and direction

At the bottom of the window, tap on **Options**. Drag the **Duration** slider to set whether the effect will be longer or shorter.

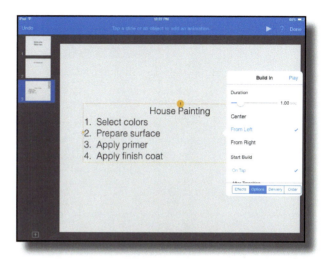

Set the starting point

Scroll down If necessary until you see available **Start Build** options. These determine when you want the animation to begin:

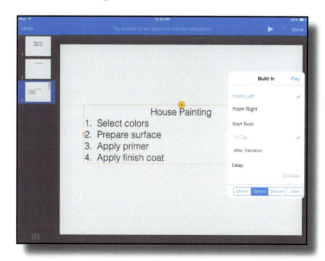

- **On Tap** begins the animation when you tap on the object.

- **After Transition** begins the effect a certain time after the slide is displayed. Use the **Delay** slider to set the delay.

Tap on **Delivery**. You can elect to build the transition in these ways:

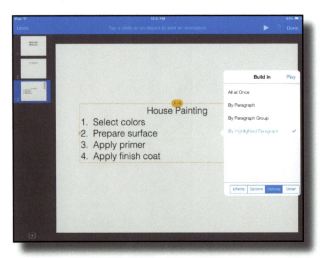

- **All at Once** delivers all your selected items in a single motion.

- **By Paragraph** builds the display one paragraph at a time.

- **By Highlighted Paragraph** highlights each paragraph as it appears on the screen.

Make your choice; then, tap on **Display** to see the results.

Chapter 11. Display your presentation.

Of course, the reason to develop a presentation is to show it to someone. You can show it on the iPad itself. Or, you can use the iPad as a controller as you display the presentation on a TV set or desktop computer.

68. Control a manual presentation

Tap on the **Tools** icon; then, select **Presentation Tools** and **Presentation Type**. Choose **Normal**

This choice activates a manual presentation. Start with an opening slide, and tap every time you want to change slides.

A **Links Only** presentation is a special type of manual display. It advances slides whenever you tap on a designated link in the display.

To start, select the slide you plan to begin with. Tap on the triangular arrow in the upper right-hand corner of the screen. .

The slide show begins. To move to the next slide, tap the display or swipe to the left.

Go back

To return to a previous slide, swipe to the right.

If you are playing the presentation on an external display, a presenter display will appear on the iPad screen. For more on using it to control the presentation, see *"72. Move a presentation to another device"*

149

Jump to another slide

If the current slide is part of an animated build, this will return you to the first slide in the build. See *"67. Build a list item by item"*.

To jump to another slide outside the presentation sequence, tap or swipe inward from the left-hand side of the display. The Slide Navigator opens.

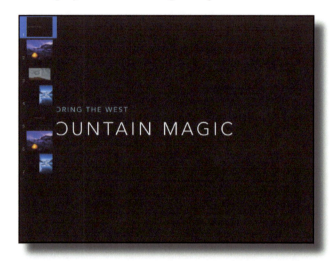

In the Navigator, tap on the slide you want to display. To close the Navigator, tap anywhere in the display. Tap again to advance the slide.

To close the presentation, pinch on the display.

69. Display a self-running presentation

Tap on the **Tools** icon; then, tap on **Presentation Tools** and **Presentation Type**. Tap on **Self-Playing**. With this selection, the presentation runs automatically like a movie.

Start the presentation

Select the slide you want to begin the presentation. Tap on the right-facing arrow in the upper right-hand corner of the screen. The presentation runs automatically through the final slide.

Refine the presentation

The Presentation Type window also includes several options you can apply to customize the presentation.

- Select **Loop Presentation to** repeat the presentation when it reaches the end. This can be useful, for example, if you want to leave the presentation on display at a trade show.

- Select **Restart Show if Idle** to restart the presentation if there is no on-screen activity over a certain time. Use this to resent the show if a viewer runs through part of the presentation but abandons it unfinished.

70. Display on a bigger screen

Sometimes it's a good idea to show a presentation on the iPad. You'll usually do this to an audience of one or two, lending itself to a personal, intimate display.

To reach a larger audience, though, you'll want to display the presentation on a larger screen. Options include a projector or Apple TV with AirPlay.

With the right connectors and adapters— these vary with the type of installation—you can use the iPad as a tool to manage the presentation while it plays on the larger screen.

Start the presentation

Connect the iPad to the external display. Tap the triangular arrow that starts the presentation.

The presentation starts on the outside display. Meanwhile, the iPad switches to a *Presenter* display with which you can manage the presentation. The presenter runs on the iPad while the presentation appears on the external display.

As you advance through the slides, the Presenter displays the slide numbers along with red and green "traffic lights" that tell you when it's safe to advance to the next slide.

Exercise options

Options for the Presenter include varying the display. You can show the current slide, the next slide, or both. The Presenter also includes a time display. Tap it to switch between a clock that shows the current time and a timer that shows the elapsed time of the presentation.

71. Print a presentation

The iPad doesn't readily handle printing. It requires that you have an active printer on your desktop—or at least somewhere—and that it is properly set up to receive printing orders from the iPad. Different printers use different methods; follow the instructions that came with your printer.

Set up the print job

AirPrint printers are equipped to process output from an iPad. These are mainly newer models.

Tap on the **Tools** button. Then, tap on **Print**. The **Layout Options** dialog box opens.

You can print each slide on a full page, or with text and other slides. Make your choice, and select whether to print builds and backgrounds. Then, tap on **Next**.

Select a printer, specify the pages to be printed and the number of copies you want to print. When ready, tap on **Print**.

72. Move a presentation to another device

iCloud is an online service that, when properly set up, stores your presentations and makes them available to your desktop computer or to other IOS devices.

The main advantage comes when you use more than one device to edit a presentation. The iCloud always maintains the latest version. When you edit the presentation on one device, then open it on another, the second device will display the latest edits from the original device.

Set up the iPad

To make use of the iCloud connection, you must make sure the iPad and Keynote to use the service.

Start by opening the **Settings** on the iPad. In the list of settings, select **iCloud**. Make sure **Documents & Data** is switched on.

If not, tap **Documents & Data**, and tap the **ON** button.

Then, scroll down to the **Applications** section and select **Keynote**. Make sure **Use iCloud** is switched on.

With these settings, when you close the presentation it will be saved on iCloud and made available to all your IOS devices.

Open the presentation on your computer

If you close a presentation while you aren't connected to the Internet, an arrow will appear in the presentation thumbnail. The presentation will be uploaded next time the iPad connects to the Internet.

If you are running the Mountain Lion or later version of OSX, the presentation will be automatically available to the iCloud version of Keynote. Use your Web browser to open *icloud.com* and sign in. A list of available applications is displayed.

Select **Keynote**. The iCloud version of Keynote displays your presentations from the iPad version.

Select a presentation. It opens in the iCloud version of
Keynote. You can edit or run it as you would on the
ipad.

Index

www.ingramcontent.com/pod-product-compliance
Lightning Source LLC
Chambersburg PA
CBHW041141050326
40689CB00001B/434

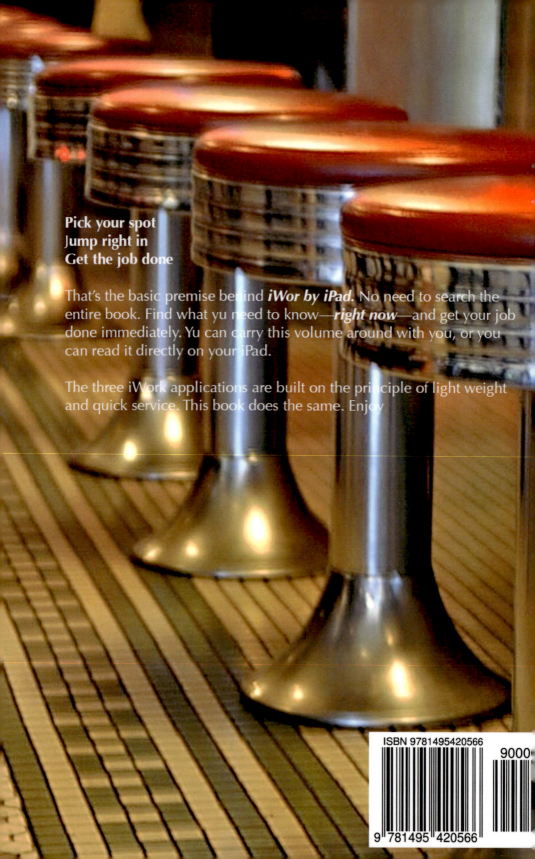

Pick your spot
Jump right in
Get the job done

That's the basic premise behind *iWor by iPad.* No need to search the entire book. Find what yu need to know—*right now*—and get your job done immediately. Yu can carry this volume around with you, or you can read it directly on your iPad.

The three iWork applications are built on the principle of light weight and quick service. This book does the same. Enjoy

ISBN 9781495420566

9000

9 781495 420566